FISHING SKILLS

D1079536

Inshore Boat Fishing

Tony Whieldon

Introduction by Russ Symons

WARD LOCK LIMITED · LONDON

© Ward Lock Limited 1985

First published in Great Britain in 1985
by Ward Lock Limited, 82 Gower Street,
London WC1E 6EQ.

Printed and bound in Italy by
New Interlitho, Milan

British Library Cataloguing in Publication Data

Whieldon, Tony
    Inshore boat fishing. — (Fishing skills)
    1. Saltwater fishing — Great Britain
    I. Title   II. Series
    799.1′6′0947   SH605

    ISBN 0-7063-6398-1

Contents

Acknowledgements
My thanks to Michael for his
assistance with the diagrams.

Introduction

Sea anglers are a breed apart from normal people; and those who own their own boats, and fish the often prolific inshore waters of Britain's coastline, are a hard-headed, self-reliant group of anglers. They know that often life itself is dependant on their own skill as amateur navigators/seamen, and how well they have prepared, even built, the boat that they take to sea. In everything they do, a streak of independence can be clearly seen.

Most boat-owning anglers started off aboard a professionally-skippered charter boat. It was aboard such boats that the joy of being afloat, experiencing the realities of the elements and pursuing one of man's oldest and most honourable tasks, the catching of fish, touched a chord deep inside the subconscious. It is unfortunate in many respects that to compete on the charter boat scene today, such boats have to be big, fast and superbly equipped and often very expensive, putting regular trips beyond the purse of anglers who want to fish at least once a week.

One advantage of inshore boat angling is that angling boats between 12 and 18 ft (in length) are easily trailed behind the average family saloon, opening up a reasonable radius of weekend fishing trips, as well as holiday trips to places beyond the scope of normal activities.

This increased mobility allows the committed angler to chase different species throughout their seasons. Winter is the time for flounders in the estuaries. Then, as spring comes upon us, bass can be found in the rocky outcrops where they begin their inshore migration. Bass continue to be found in summer, and in addition the reefs harbour pollack. And as autumn evenings begin to close in on us, rays can be tempted off the bottom.

Another aspect of inshore boat angling is the fact that you can fish any way you want without attracting disparaging remarks from those who think they know better, or getting involved with the proverbial 'tangler' who, despite all advice, will without appearing to try, succeed in tangling every line that is in the water. Often because of this freedom of action, anglers are more likely to match the strength of their tackle to the weight, strength and vigour of the species which they seek.

The reward for the small boat angler is not measured by the sackful of dead fish, but rather in the inward satisfaction of knowing that he or she has 'put it together'; the boat has been taken to the right place, it has performed in proportion to the effort expended in making sure that it was utterly seaworthy, and the right bait was used on tackle chosen to give good sport.

Angling 'experts' are viewed with a jaundiced eye by the majority of anglers, but those who can put their experience to intelligent and thoughtful use will catch fish more often than others who just 'hope for the best'. And the small boat angler is probably better placed to acquire this experience than anglers who rely on a charter boat skipper's knowledge.

One of Britain's best known and most successful charter skippers, who gained his background in a small boat, once said to me in an unguarded moment, that he goes over better fishing on the way out to the distant, deep-water wrecks, than often those same wrecks have to offer, but that it takes 'real anglers' to catch the inshore fish.

This book seeks to encourage these self-same 'real anglers', and for that it deserves real praise.

Russ Symons,
Plymouth, Devon.

February 1985.

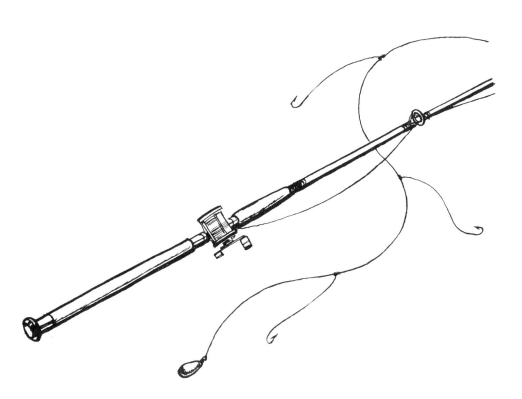

Popular inshore species

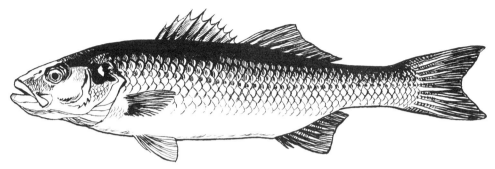

BASS It is probably true to say that more inshore anglers pursue this fish than any other species. Bass are fine sporting fish, and make excellent eating.

Because of the heavy toll taken by commercial netsmen over the years the bass population has been drastically reduced. The thoughtful angler will help to ease this situation by returning to the sea all undersized bass.

The bass is a very catholic feeder, voraciously consuming crustaceans, small fish and worms. Preoccupation with one particular food item may occur in certain areas; for example, where a large shoal of bait-fish such as sandeels or pilchards exist. Care should be taken when handling a bass, for the dorsal fin and gill covers bristle with many sharp spines.

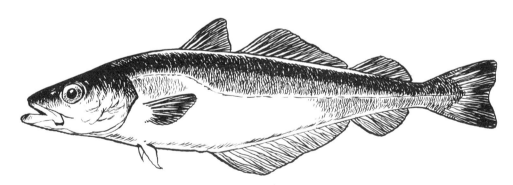

POLLACK Another fine sporting fish which is also good to eat if freshly caught. Less of a roamer than the bass, it prefers to swim and hunt close to rocky under-water pinnacles. However, a large shoal of bait-fish such as sandeels will tempt the pollack into open water, but the bulk of its diet consists mainly of crustaceans and small fish which rely on the shelter of rocky surroundings.

MACKEREL

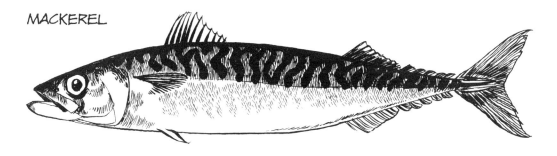

This game little fish provides sport par excellence, tastes delicious and is a first-class bait for most other species.

During the warmer months, huge shoals come to within inches of the shoreline in their frenzy to feed on small fry.

GARFISH Wherever a shoal of mackerel is active near the surface, garfish will almost certainly be present. They feed on small fish, which are seized in the sharp-toothed, beak-like jaws. They provide plenty of action on light gear, but from the culinary point of view leave much to be desired.

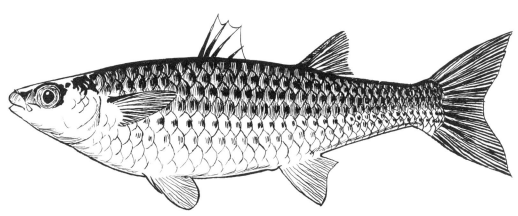

GREY MULLET For sheer cunning, a good turn of speed and stamina, the grey mullet has it all. Contrary to some opinions, the flesh is good to eat if well seasoned with herbs.

The following species are valued more for their eating qualities than as sporting fish. They range in size from the tiny ½ lb (0·25kg) dab to the massive turbot which can weigh 30lb (14kg) or more.

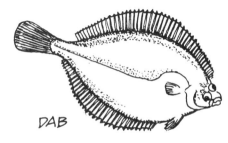

DAB

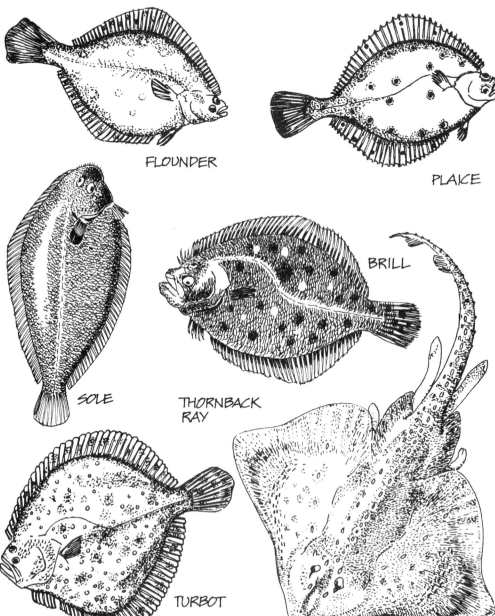

FLOUNDER

PLAICE

SOLE

THORNBACK
RAY

BRILL

TURBOT

Location

Rocks and reefs

BASS

GREY MULLET

BLACK BREAM

RED BREAM

POLLACK

BALLAN WRASSE

Sandbanks

BASS

Sand and gravel banks

PLAICE

TURBOT

BRILL

Sand and mud

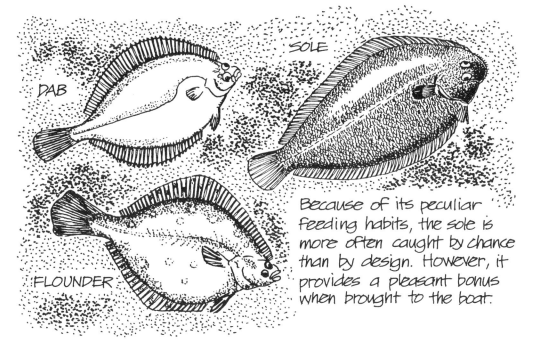

Because of its peculiar feeding habits, the sole is more often caught by chance than by design. However, it provides a pleasant bonus when brought to the boat.

Sand, mud and gravel

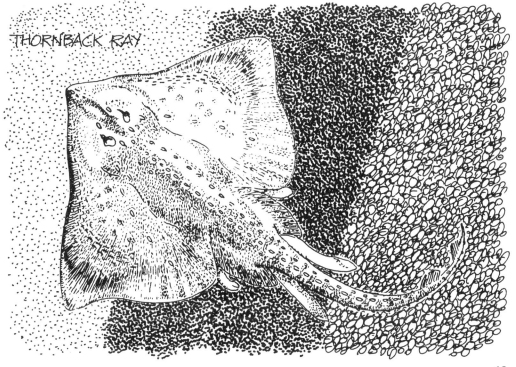

Rough bottom

Open water (summer)

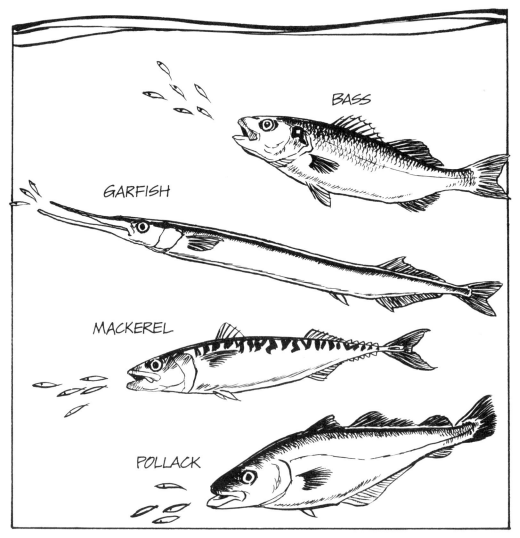

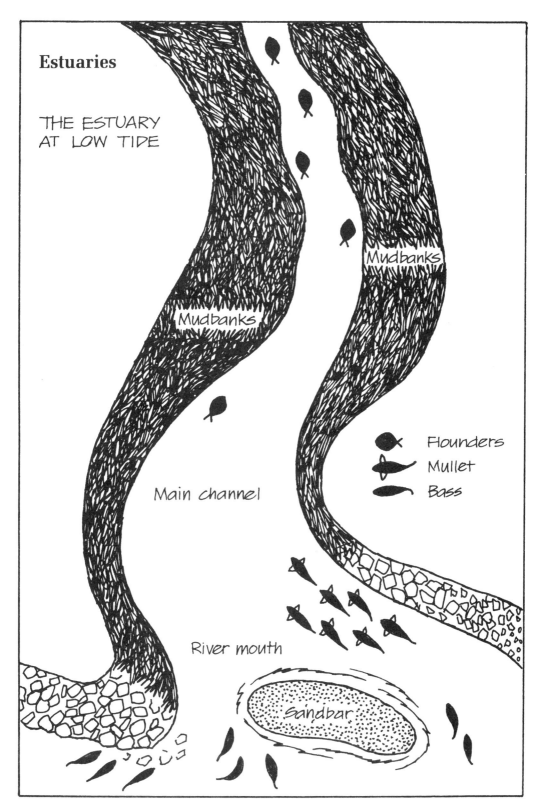

Estuaries

THE ESTUARY
AT LOW TIDE

Mudbanks

Mudbanks

Main channel

Flounders
Mullet
Bass

River mouth

Sandbar

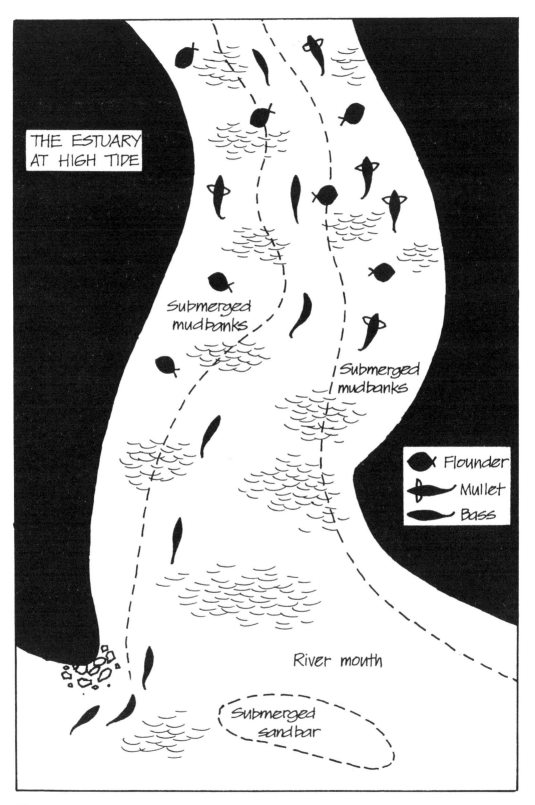

THE ESTUARY AT HIGH TIDE

Submerged mudbanks

Submerged mudbanks

Flounder
Mullet
Bass

River mouth

Submerged sandbar

During the period between low tide and high tide any form of obstruction situated in the path of the tidal flow will create, on its sheltered side, a haven for smaller creatures, on which larger fish will feed. Any such obstruction is always worth investigation. Here are a few examples.

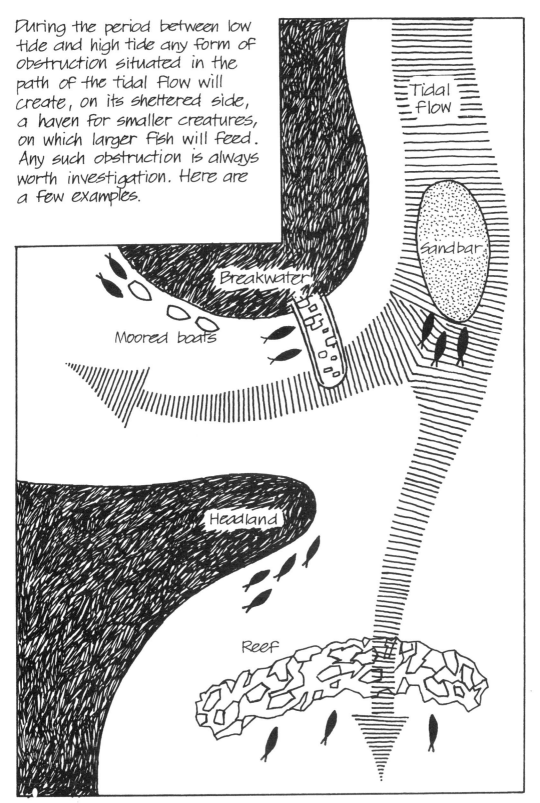

Tidal Flow

Sandbar

Breakwater

Moored boats

Headland

Reef

Rods

The single-handed spinning rod (top) is the ideal tool for flicking a small artificial lure to fish which are feeding near the surface. Bass, mackerel and garfish often chase small fry in the upper layers of the water, and with this little rod the angler can appreciate the fine fighting qualities of these fish to the full. The reel best suited to this rod would be a fixed-spool type loaded with line of about 8lb(3·05kg) breaking strain.

The centre rod is a 20lb(9kg) boat rod which is suitable for the majority of inshore species. To be on the safe side, and considering loss of line strength through abrasion on rocks, gravel and the like, a line with a breaking strain of not less than 18lb(8kg) should be used. The length of this rod will be about 7ft 6ins(2·30m), and is the backbone of the inshore boat angler's armoury. It is used, in conjunction with a multiplier reel, to fish natural or artificial baits in deeper areas of water. Fibreglass is probably the most practical material when one considers the amount of rough treatment to which this rod may be subjected.

The bottom rod is a 10ft(3·05m) model(sometimes known as an up-tide rod) for casting natural baits when fishing from an anchored boat over the shallower areas of open sea and estuary. It is also ideal for trolling artificial lures, the extra length being beneficial for holding the line well away from the side of the boat.

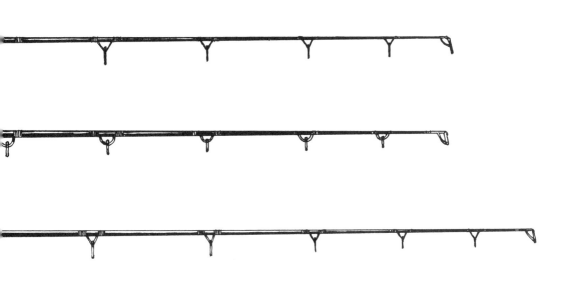

Reels

SKIRTED FIXED-SPOOL
For use with a spinning rod; for casting lures, very light bait fishing, and float fishing. Loaded with 8lb (3·05kg) monofilament line.

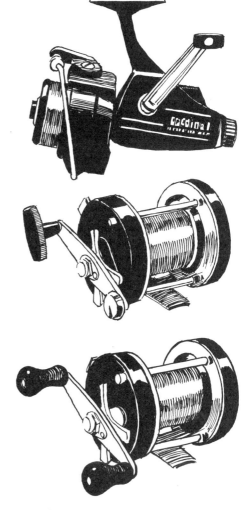

BOAT MULTIPLIER
Companion for the 20lb (9kg) boat rod. Used for general boat work and loaded with 18lb (8kg) monofilament line.

BOATCASTING MULTIPLIER
For up-tide fishing and lighter general boat fishing. Loaded with 10lb (4·50kg) monofilament line.

Up-tide fishing

This method is best suited to the comparatively shallow waters of estuaries, or over shallow, clean areas just offshore.

The bait — peeler, worm or fish — is cast up-tide from an anchored boat. Species caught by this method include bass, rays, flounders and plaice.

A paternoster is the best sort of terminal rig for up-tiding.

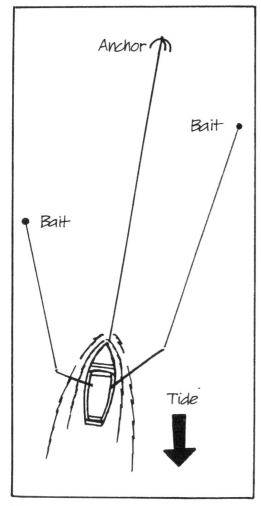

Anchor

Bait

Bait

Tide

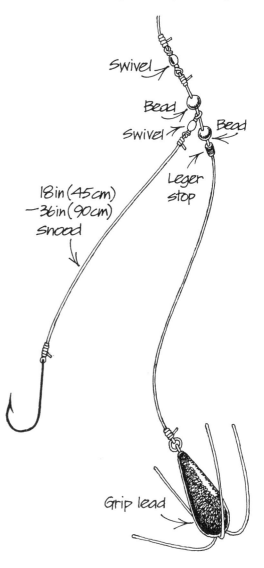

Swivel

Bead

Swivel

Bead

Leger stop

18in (45cm) —36in (90cm) snood

Grip lead

Fishing with the up-tide method is usually more productive than fishing over the stern of the boat, because noise and vibrations are carried, by the tide, away from the area where the bait is fished.

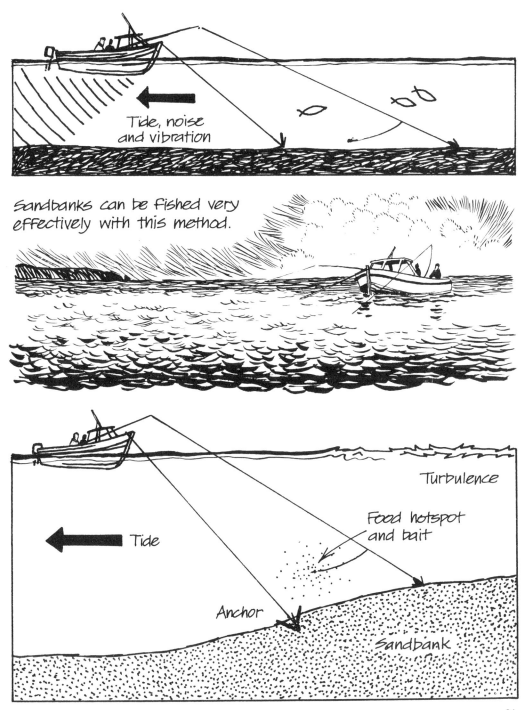

Tide, noise and vibration

Sandbanks can be fished very effectively with this method.

Turbulence

Food hotspot and bait

Tide

Anchor

Sandbank

Float fishing close to rocks

The ideal way to present a bait close to rocks is to suspend it beneath a float. This method will minimize the risk of losing end tackle, and will impart a natural movement to the bait as the tidal currents and eddies swirl around the rocks.

When fishing close to rocks it is an advantage to use a rod with a good length in order to control a hooked fish; the rod used for up-tide work is ideal.

Fishing close to rocks should only be practised when the sea is calm.

Stop knot

Sliding float

Swivel

Drilled bullet

Adjust the sliding stop knot to the deepest possible position, the idea being to present the bait (ragworm, crab or prawn) just clear of the rocks.

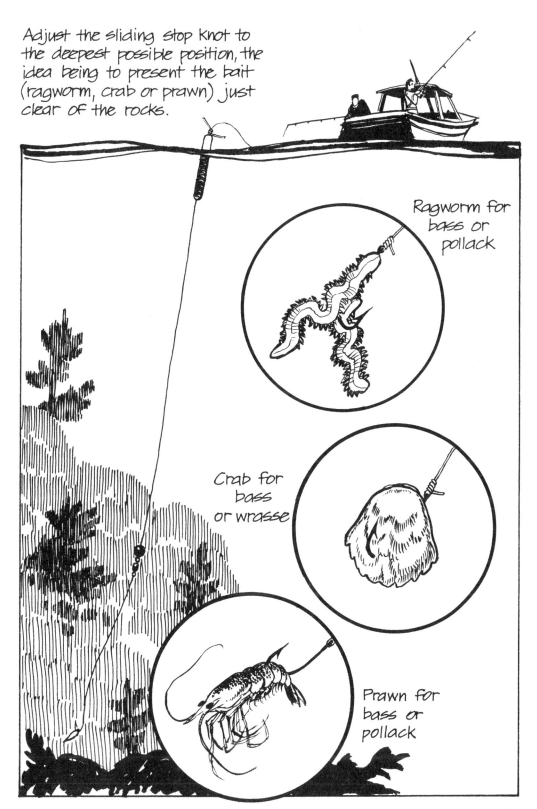

Ragworm for bass or pollack

Crab for bass or wrasse

Prawn for bass or pollack

Sometimes pollack will take the bait as the tackle is being retrieved. The angler should be prepared for this — the first rush of a hooked pollack tests both tackle and angler.

Some anglers attach a spoon or spinner above the bait in order to encourage pollack to strike on the retrieve.

Spinning over a reef

By cutting the engine, the boat is allowed to drift over the area of the reef. The lure is then cast, with the aid of a spinning rod, and allowed to sink to the required depth. It is then retrieved in a sink-and-draw motion. Bass are often caught this way, and pollack will also take a lure fished in this manner.

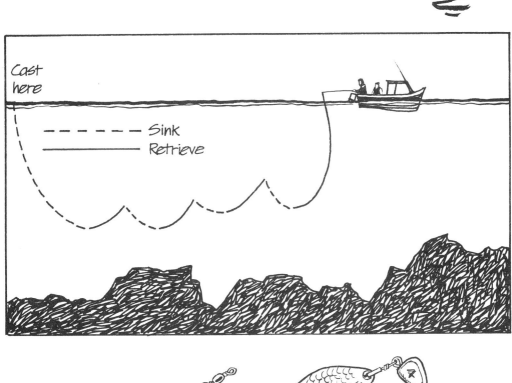

Cast here

- - - - - Sink
——— Retrieve

TOBY
For bass

LAURENS SPOON
For pollack

The paternoster

The paternoster is a versatile and invaluable rig to all boat anglers. The modern trend in paternosters is towards simplicity — moving away from the old designs, which often incorporated enough brass and steel wire booms almost to cause the boat to list.

BASIC NYLON PATERNOSTER

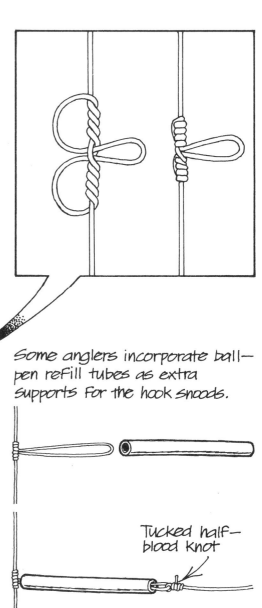

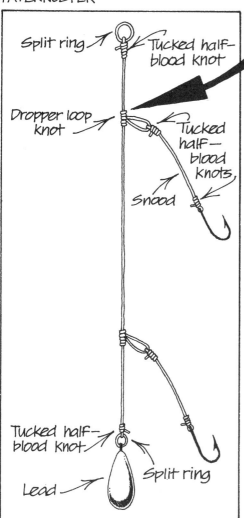

Split ring → Tucked half-blood knot

Dropper loop knot → Tucked half-blood knots,

Snood

Tucked half-blood knot →

Lead → Split ring

Some anglers incorporate ball—pen refill tubes as extra supports for the hook snoods.

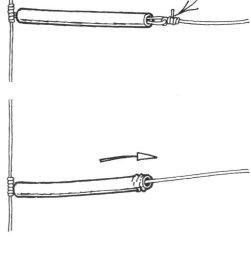

Tucked half-blood knot

Paternoster with three-way swivels

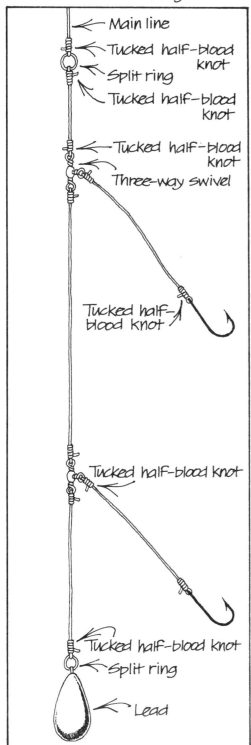

Main line

Tucked half-blood knot

Split ring

Tucked half-blood knot

Tucked half-blood knot

Three-way swivel

Tucked half-blood knot

Tucked half-blood knot

Tucked half-blood knot

Split ring

Lead

Blood knot paternoster

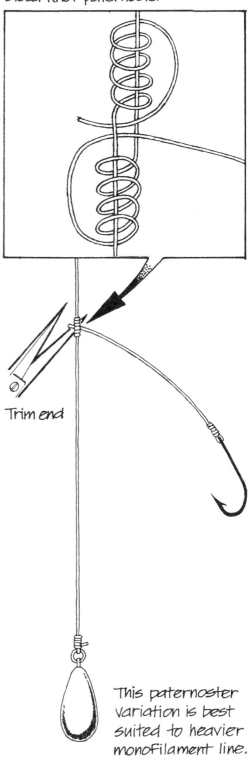

Trim end

This paternoster variation is best suited to heavier monofilament line.

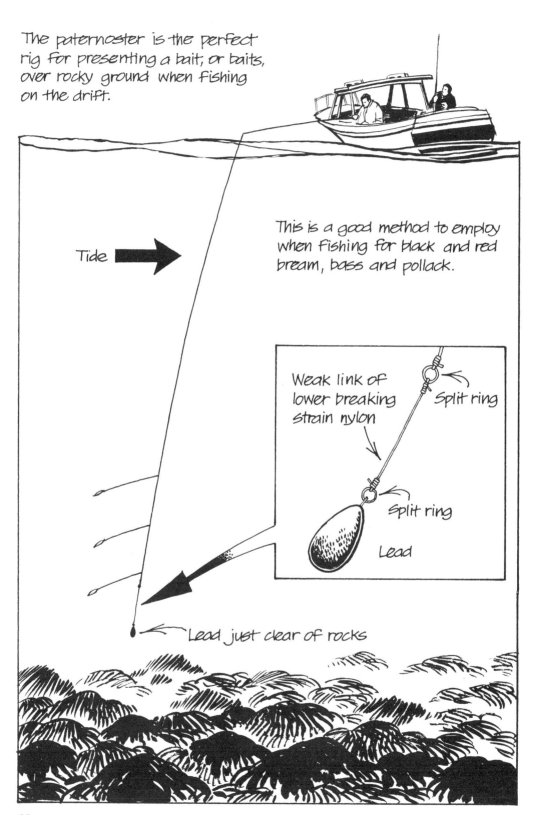

The paternoster is the perfect rig for presenting a bait; or baits, over rocky ground when fishing on the drift.

This is a good method to employ when fishing for black and red bream, bass and pollack.

Tide

Weak link of lower breaking strain nylon

Split ring

Split ring

Lead

Lead just clear of rocks

A 20 lb (9 kg) class rod should be used with a two- or three-hook paternoster, for at times it is possible to hook two or even three fish at the same time.
A multiplier reel loaded with 18 lb (8 kg) line completes the outfit.

When the tide is slack, or during neap tides, it may be necessary to connect one or two wire booms.

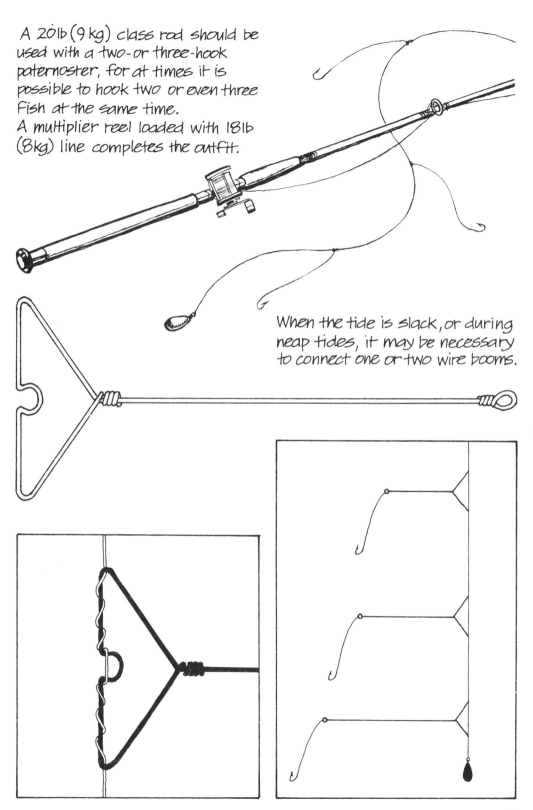

Rig for black and red bream.

If there is a good tide running, artificial lures can be used in conjunction with a paternoster.

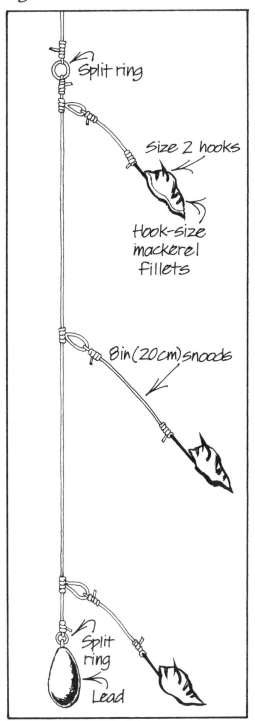

Split ring

Size 2 hooks

Hook-size mackerel fillets

8in (20cm) snoods

Split ring

Lead

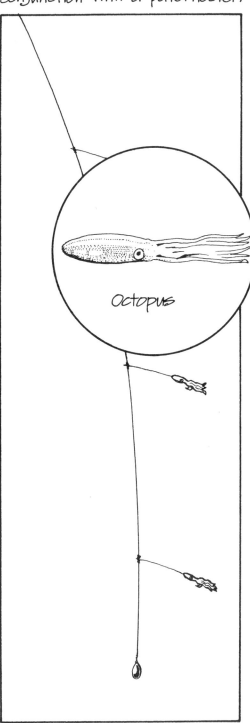

Octopus

Artificial lures tied to the ends of the snoods will attract predators, such as bass or pollack.

It is important to ensure that the snoods are spaced far enough apart to prevent tangles.

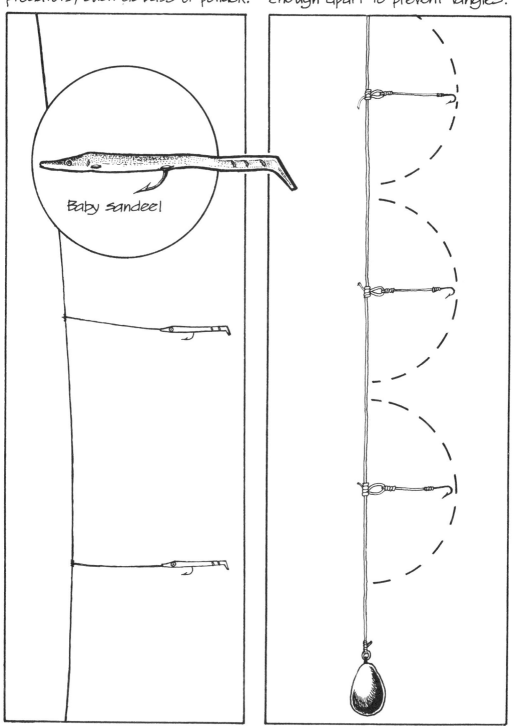

Baby sandeel

Fishing for bass

The most enjoyable way of taking this bold and sporting fish is with an artificial lure.

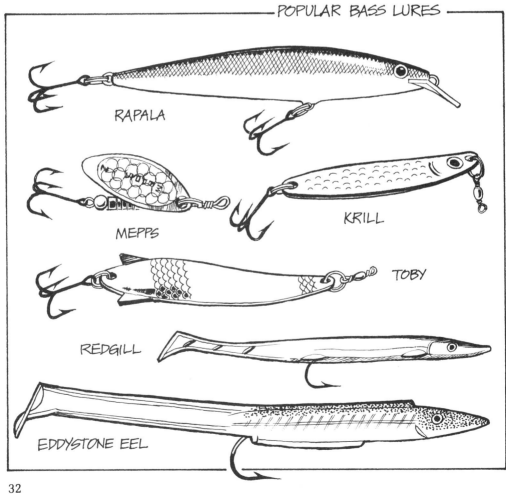

POPULAR BASS LURES

RAPALA

MEPPS

KRILL

TOBY

REDGILL

EDDYSTONE EEL

During the summer months, large shoals of small fry congregate and move close to the shoreline. Below the surface of the water bass take advantage of the easy pickings; above, seabirds such as terns and gulls have their share of the feast.

Keep a sharp look-out for birds wheeling and diving and steer the boat towards the disturbance. Proceed quietly and stop the boat well clear of the shoal.

Using a single-handed spinning rod, cast the lure beyond the area of fish activity.

By swinging the rod from side to side during the retrieve, a more natural action will be imparted to the lure, and it will then approach the boat in a zig-zag pattern, very typical of a wounded or panic-stricken bait fish.

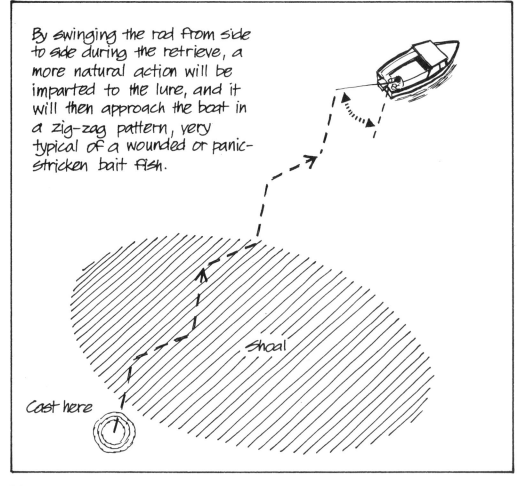

Shoal

Cast here

The majority of lures for this
type of fishing are heavy enough
in themselves, but extra weight may
be needed for fishing artificial
sandeels, or fishing at greater
depth. This can be provided by
using a foldover lead or a Wye lead.

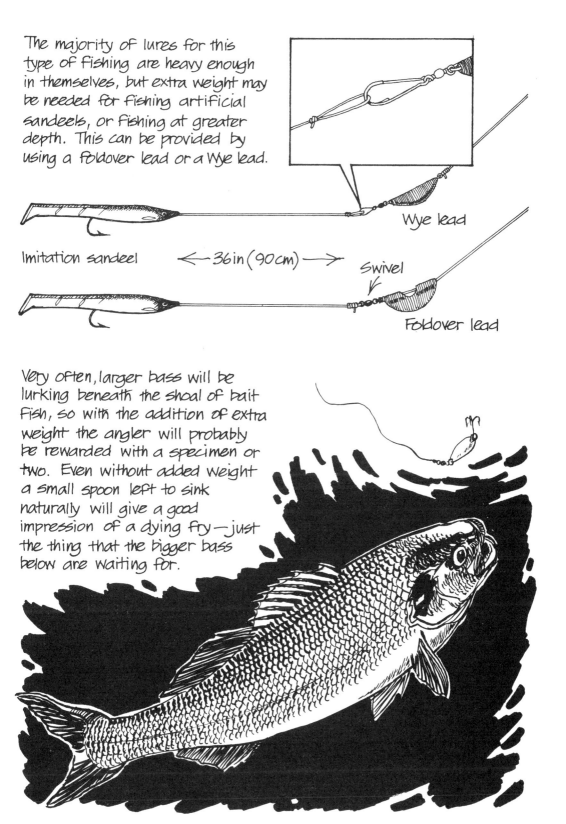

Wye lead

Imitation sandeel   ←—36in (90cm)—→   Swivel

Foldover lead

Very often, larger bass will be
lurking beneath the shoal of bait
fish, so with the addition of extra
weight the angler will probably
be rewarded with a specimen or
two. Even without added weight
a small spoon left to sink
naturally will give a good
impression of a dying fry—just
the thing that the bigger bass
below are waiting for.

Trolling for bass

Bass will also be found lurking around jagged reefs. Reference to an Admiralty chart will disclose the whereabouts of such places, which sometimes rise from the seabed almost to the surface, and in some cases above it.

Reefs can be dangerous places for the inexperienced. The prudent angler, therefore, should always be in the company of someone who is conversant with the local rocks, and then only during settled weather conditions.

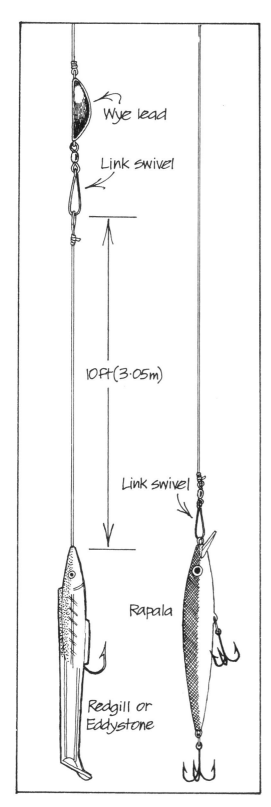

Wye lead

Link swivel

10ft (3·05m)

Link swivel

Rapala

Redgill or Eddystone

Imitation sandeels and Rapala lures are ideal for trolling. The sandeel will need extra weight to hold it down, but the Rapala can be tied directly to the line. The diving vane on the front of the lure will cause it to dive.

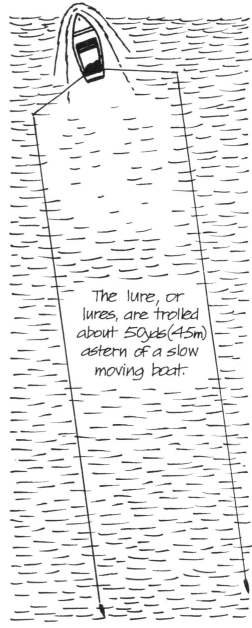

The lure, or lures, are trolled about 50yds (45m) astern of a slow moving boat.

The rod will need to be supported in some way during trolling until a fish hits the lure.

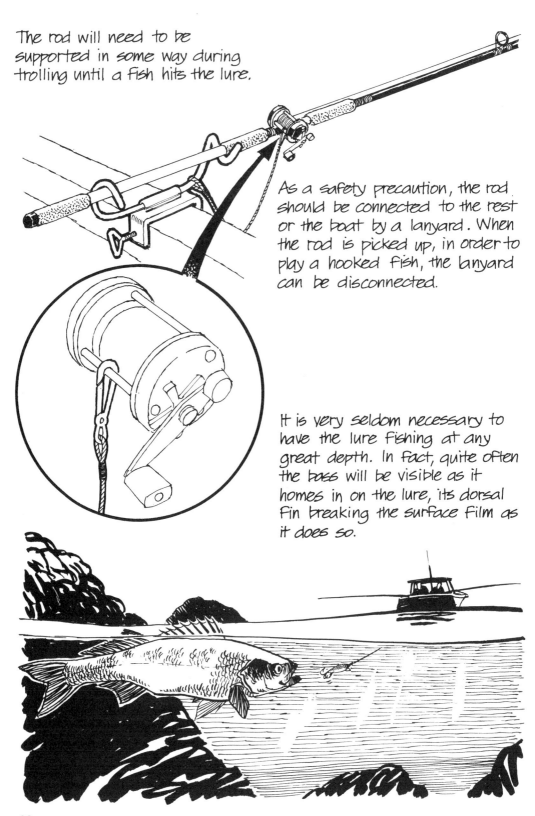

As a safety precaution, the rod should be connected to the rest or the boat by a lanyard. When the rod is picked up, in order to play a hooked fish, the lanyard can be disconnected.

It is very seldom necessary to have the lure fishing at any great depth. In fact, quite often the bass will be visible as it homes in on the lure, its dorsal fin breaking the surface film as it does so.

Driftlining for bass

This method is employed from a boat which is anchored up-tide of a sand bank. The bait most commonly used is a live sandeel.

Method for mounting sandeel

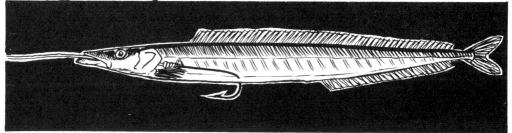

The best way of keeping sandeels alive and healthy is to put them in a wooden courge. The courge is then tethered to the boat by a lanyard and put into the water.

An alternative method is to put the sandeels in a bucket of fresh sea-water which has a battery-operated aerator attached.

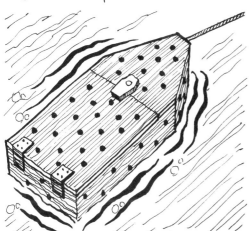

Some additional weight is usually required to hold the sandeel down, but this should be kept to a minimum to retain as natural a presentation as possible.

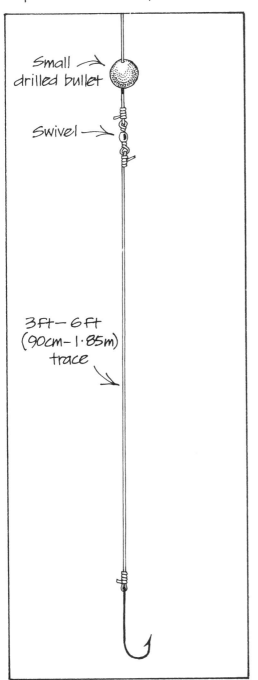

Small drilled bullet

Swivel

3ft — 6ft (90cm—1.85m) trace

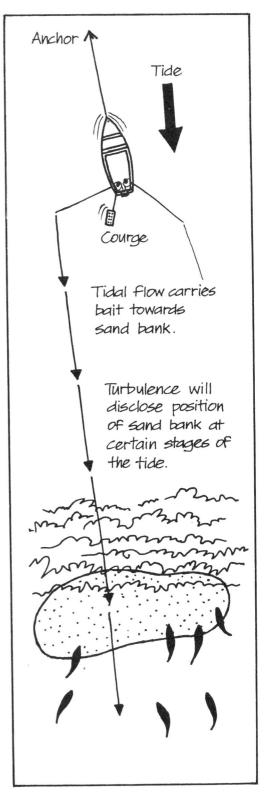

Anchor

Tide

Courge

Tidal flow carries bait towards sand bank.

Turbulence will disclose position of sand bank at certain stages of the tide.

Driftlining can be employed in many estuary mouths. The boat is allowed to drift with the tidal current, with the line and bait flowing out before the boat in a most natural manner.

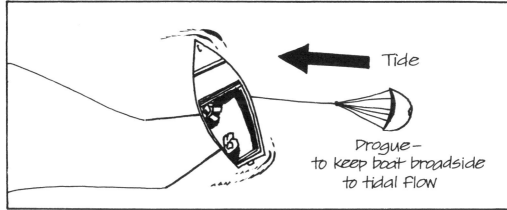

Tide

Drogue —
to keep boat broadside
to tidal flow

When a bass takes the bait, it should be given some slack line before the strike is made ....

① ②

.... then flick the reel into the 'on' position, pause for a second and lift the rod smoothly.

The driftline method can also be used to fish a prawn close to rocks. The prawn should be allowed to drift around naturally in the tidal eddies, therefore little or no lead will be required.

Fine wire Aberdeen hook

Prawns can be caught in a drop-net which is baited with scraps of fish. They can then be kept alive in a bucket of fresh sea-water which must be well oxygenated with an aerator pump.

How to catch prawns

Choose a spot with a snag-free bottom, with a fair depth of water, and close to rocks or a harbour wall. Lower the net to the bottom, wait for approximately five minutes, then draw the net quickly to the surface.

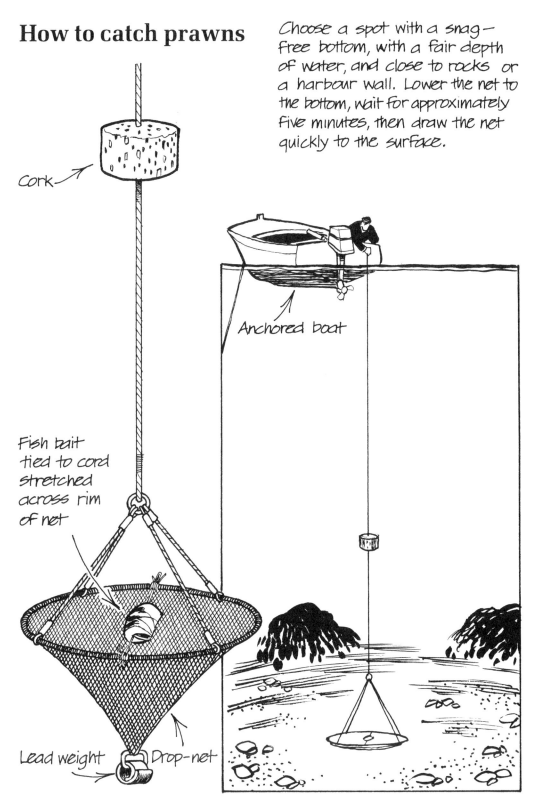

Cork

Fish bait tied to cord stretched across rim of net

Anchored boat

Lead weight

Drop-net

Reef fishing for pollack

Reef pollack can be caught by spinning, but a natural bait presented on a long, flowing trace is far more productive.

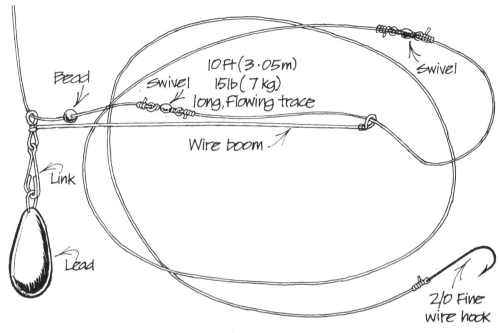

Bead

Swivel

10ft (3.05m)
15lb (7 kg)
long, flowing trace

Swivel

Wire boom

Link

Lead

2/0 fine wire hook

The finest bait for reef pollack is a live sandeel.

A 20lb (9kg) boat rod and a multiplier reel complete the outfit.

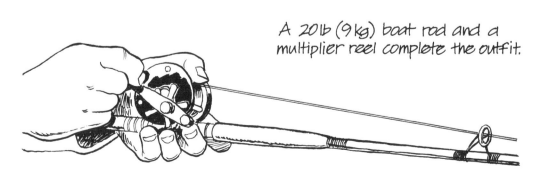

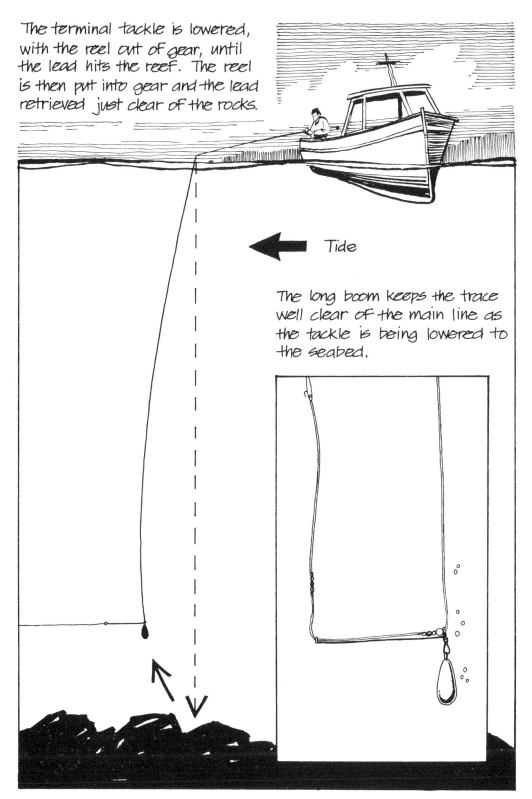

The terminal tackle is lowered, with the reel out of gear, until the lead hits the reef. The reel is then put into gear and the lead retrieved just clear of the rocks.

Tide

The long boom keeps the trace well clear of the main line as the tackle is being lowered to the seabed.

If live sandeel is not available a <u>small</u> imitation can be used

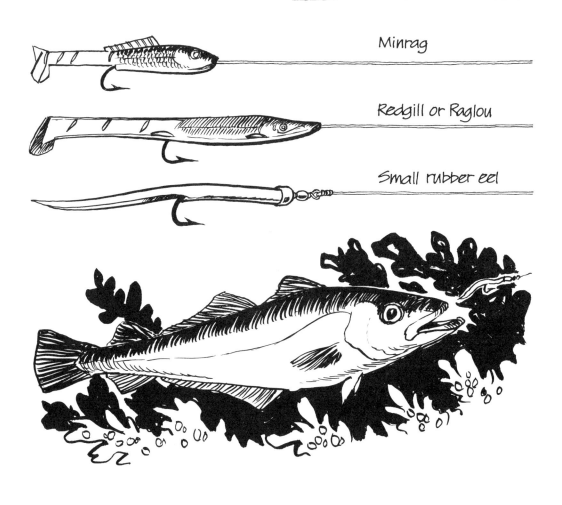

Minrag

Redgill or Raglou

Small rubber eel

Other good reef pollack baits

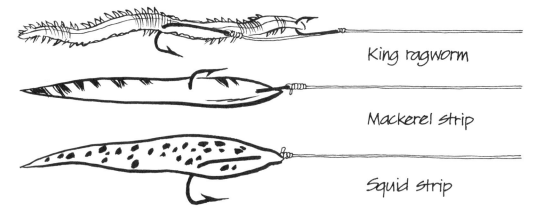

King ragworm

Mackerel strip

Squid strip

Fishing for ray

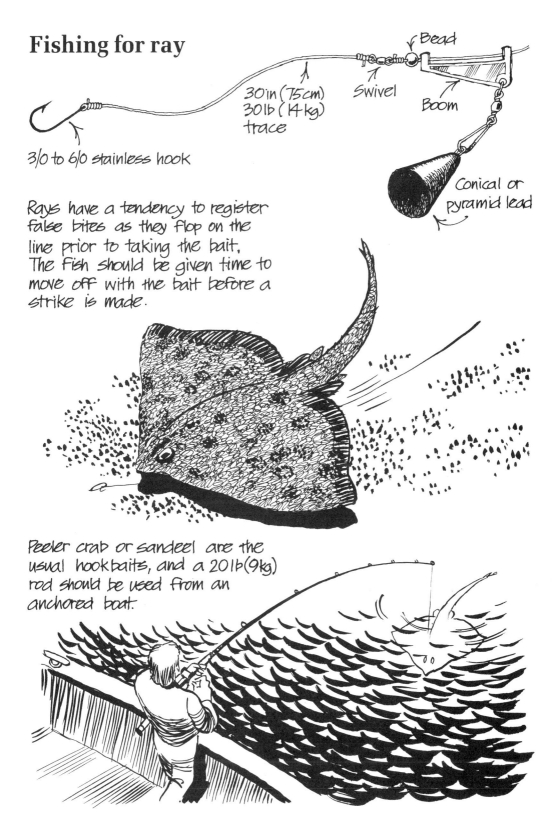

Bead

Swivel

Boom

30 in (75cm)
30 lb (14 kg)
trace

3/0 to 6/0 stainless hook

Conical or
pyramid lead

Rays have a tendency to register
false bites as they flop on the
line prior to taking the bait.
The fish should be given time to
move off with the bait before a
strike is made.

Peeler crab or sandeel are the
usual hookbaits, and a 20lb(9kg)
rod should be used from an
anchored boat.

Fishing for mackerel and garfish

During the summer, mackerel move inshore and harry shoals of small fry near the surface.

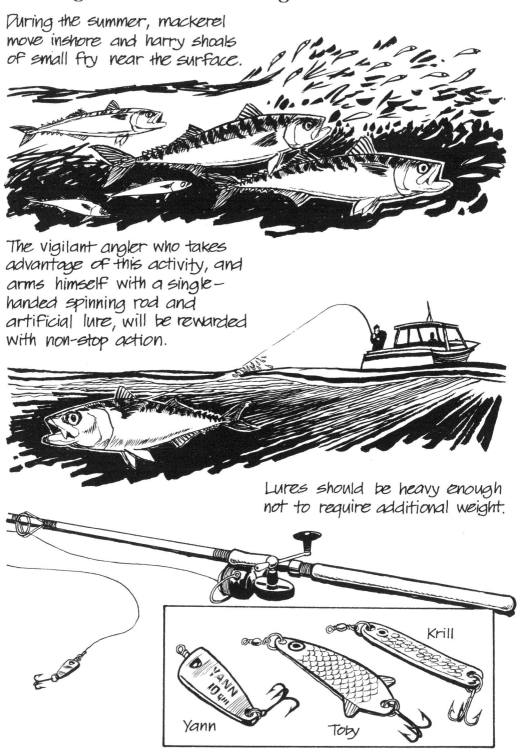

The vigilant angler who takes advantage of this activity, and arms himself with a single-handed spinning rod and artificial lure, will be rewarded with non-stop action.

Lures should be heavy enough not to require additional weight.

YANN
10 gm

Yann

Toby

Krill

When a shoal of feeding mackerel is sighted, the boat should be manoeuvred to a position slightly in front of the shoal, and to one side. The engine should then be put into neutral gear and the boat allowed to drift.

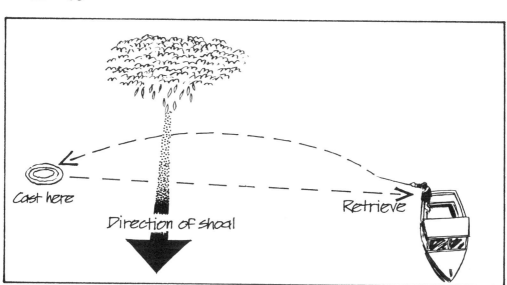

Cast here

Direction of shoal

Retrieve

The position of the boat will have to be adjusted every so often in order to keep in touch with the moving shoal. Never be tempted to take the boat too close to the shoal.

Mackerel also respond well to a float-fished bait, especially when it is fished in river mouths and harbours.

Simply let the tackle drift with the tide. It is a good policy to give the line a rub with line floatant.

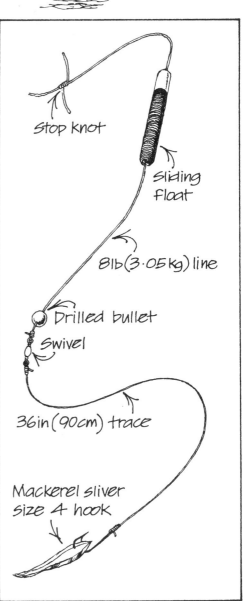

Stop knot

Sliding float

8lb (3·05kg) line

Drilled bullet

Swivel

36in (90cm) trace

Mackerel sliver size 4 hook

A net containing fish offal, tied to the stern of the boat, will create a feed lane through which to trot the float tackle.

Check the passage of the float occasionally to impart a little more attraction to the bait.

After each trot down-tide, the tackle should be retrieved very slowly — fish often take the bait at this stage.

Garfish respond particularly well to this form of fishing and will take a bait suspended only a few inches beneath the surface.

The garfish is an extrovert when it comes to taking a bait....

.... and when hooked will perform spectacular acrobatics.

Feathering for mackerel

The angler wanting to experience the fighting qualities of the mackerel should not use this method. It is useful, however, to the pot-hunter, or to the angler who needs to catch a number of mackerel quickly, in order to use them as bait for other species of fish.

A 20lb (9 kg) boat rod in conjunction with a multiplier reel is the best rod to use for this comparatively clumsy form of angling.

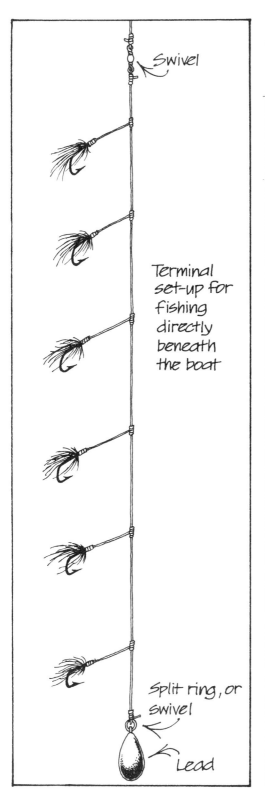

Swivel

Terminal
set-up for
fishing
directly
beneath
the boat

Split ring, or
swivel

Lead

Lower the tackle to the seabed,
then recover a little line.

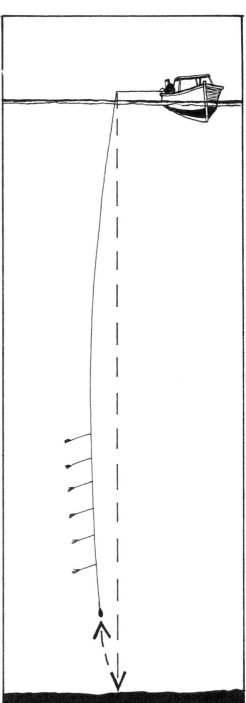

Work the feathers by raising
and lowering the rod tip.
If there is no response . . . . .

. . . . . recover more line and
continue to work the feathers.
Repeat the process until the
mackerel are located.

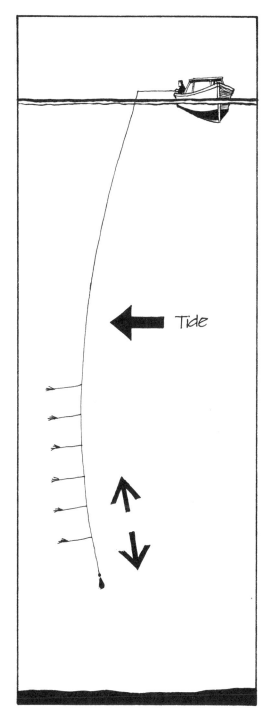

Tide

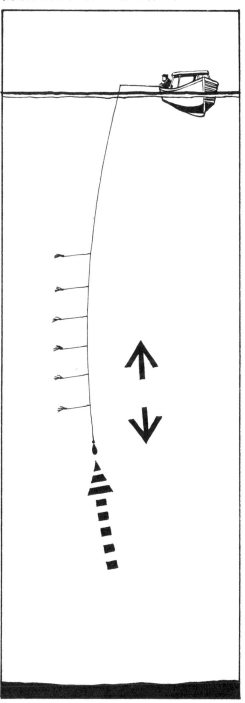

Rigs for mackerel trolling

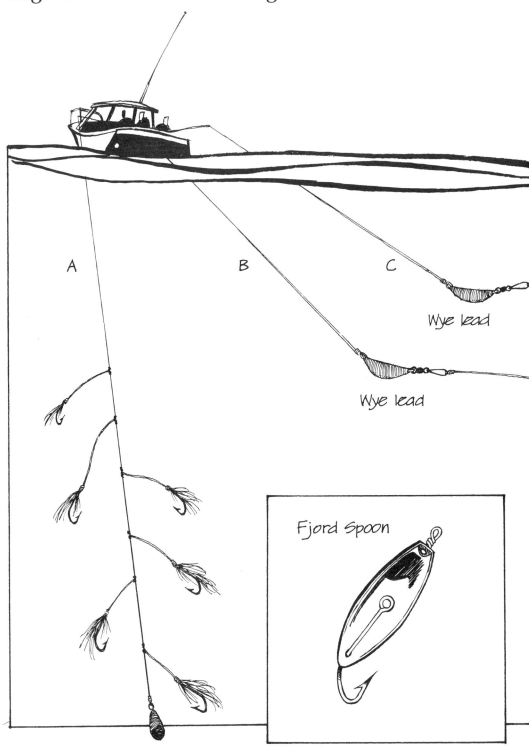

A

B

C

Wye lead

Wye lead

Fjord spoon

Rig (A) is the same set-up as that used for jigging feathers under a drifting boat. Spoons or spinners can be substituted for the feathers. This rig should be trolled very slowly in order to keep the feathers or spoons fishing at a decent angle from the line.

Rigs (B) and (C) are more suited to shallower water and should be trolled about 50yds (45m) astern of the boat.
Handlines are often used for this method of catching mackerel although more often by the casual holiday-maker than by the serious angler.

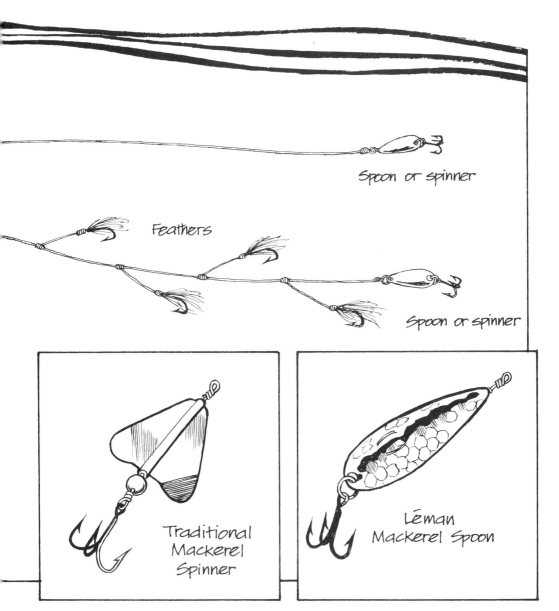

Spoon or spinner

Feathers

Spoon or spinner

Traditional Mackerel Spinner

Léman Mackerel Spoon

Fishing for grey mullet

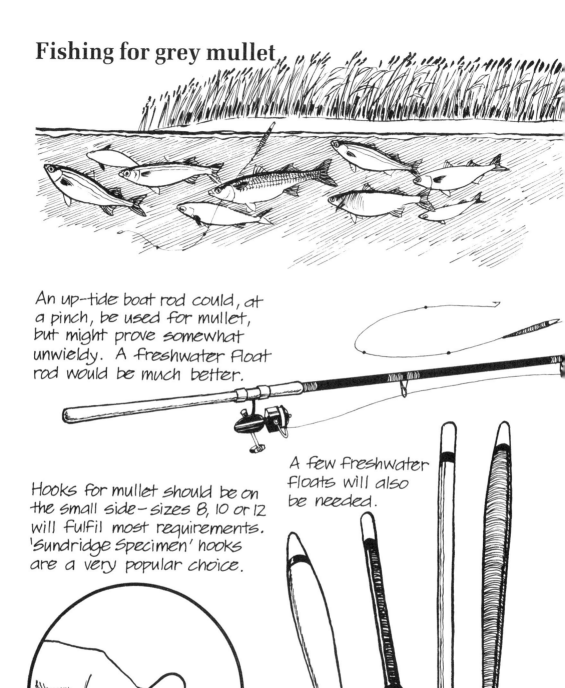

An up-tide boat rod could, at a pinch, be used for mullet, but might prove somewhat unwieldy. A freshwater float rod would be much better.

Hooks for mullet should be on the small side – sizes 8, 10 or 12 will fulfil most requirements. 'Sundridge Specimen' hooks are a very popular choice.

A few freshwater floats will also be needed.

The best areas in which to look for grey mullet are estuaries, harbours and salt-water lagoons. Shoals will move into these areas as the tide starts to flow.

The best plan of attack is to position the boat on a known mullet route just before the tide starts to flow.

Mullet will take a variety of baits.

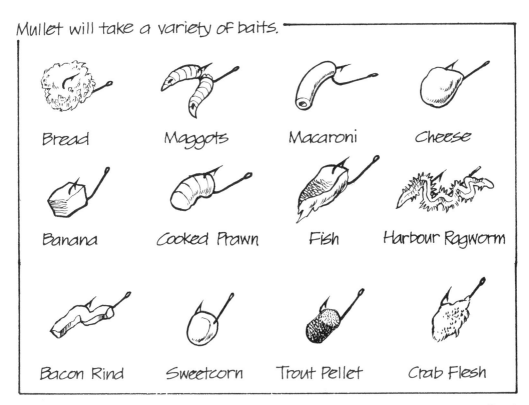

Bread

Maggots

Macaroni

Cheese

Banana

Cooked Prawn

Fish

Harbour Ragworm

Bacon Rind

Sweetcorn

Trout Pellet

Crab Flesh

Pilchard oil makes an ideal additive to most baits and loose feed.

No matter what bait the mullet angler decides to use, its effect will be enhanced by the intro-duction of a certain amount of free offerings identical to the hook bait. A meshed bag hanging under the boat, and filled with necessary samples, will ensure a constant stream of loose feed.

Maggots are best dispensed by putting them in a tin which has had holes drilled in the sides and bottom.

Float tackle is allowed to follow the tidal flow amidst the particles of loose feed.

Tide

There is no hard and fast rule on when to strike a mullet bite. These fish are wizards at playing with the bait, and will often nudge it with their top lip without actually taking it in their mouth.

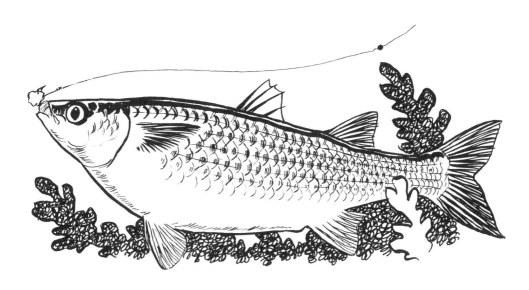

In order to keep in touch with the shoal the anchor will have to be lifted at intervals, this will allow the boat to drift up-tide.

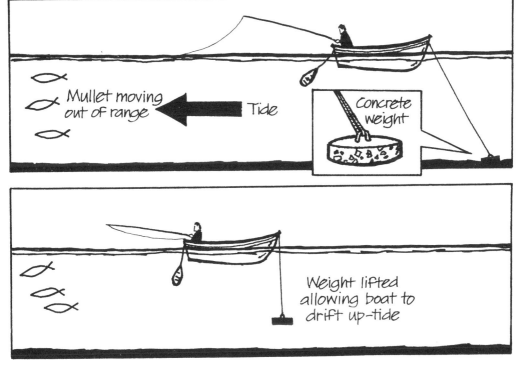

Mullet moving out of range

Tide

Concrete weight

Weight lifted allowing boat to drift up-tide

Harbours do not present as
many problems as open estuaries.
The mullet tend to stay in one
area through the duration of the
tide, so there is seldom any
need to keep moving the boat.
Mullet love to hang around
beneath cargo boats, waiting
for scraps of food.

A slow-sinking bait with most, or
all, of the weight near the float
will usually tempt these harbour
fish, which are bolder in their
feeding habits than the fish of
the estuary.

In some areas mullet are quite predatory and will attack a small spoon, especially if it is baited with harbour ragworm.

A piece of floating bread crust fished free-line, or with just a small section of peacock quill held to the line by float rubbers will also tempt mullet.

Whichever method is used to capture these powerful fish, a landing net is essential, and should always be close at hand.

Turbot and brill

Banks of sand, shell-grit or gravel provide the ideal habitat for these much sought-after species.

A 20lb (9kg) class rod is used in conjunction with a multiplier reel loaded with 18lb (8kg) line.

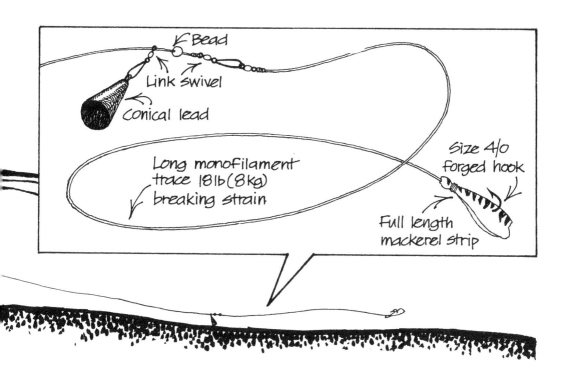

Bead

Link swivel

Conical lead

Long monofilament trace 18lb (8kg) breaking strain

Size 4/0 forged hook

Full length mackerel strip

If the tide is running strongly it might be better to fish on the drift. The disturbance of the dragging lead in the sand will help to attract the turbot and brill. It is common practice to use three hooks.

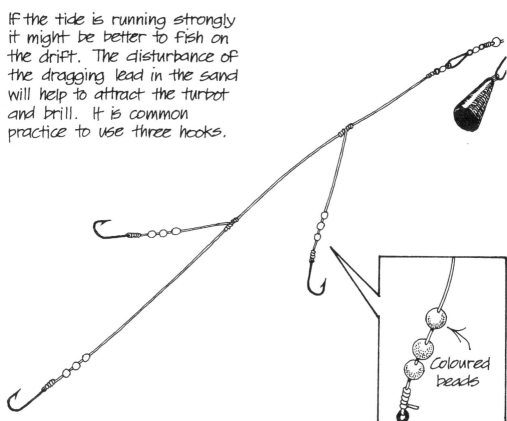

Coloured beads

Fishing for dabs

Dabs make delicious eating and provide non-stop action if a hot-spot is located. Very light tackle can be used for this little fish, which can be caught in shallow water, often directly under the boat.

A single-handed spinning rod, fixed-spool reel loaded with 8lb (3.05kg) line and basic terminal tackle is best suited for this little fish.

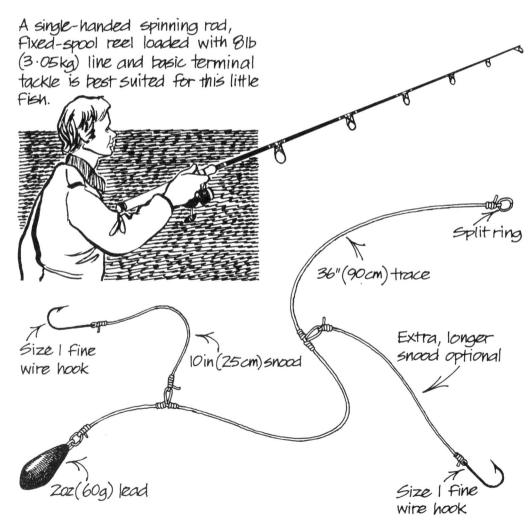

Split ring

36"(90cm) trace

Extra, longer snood optional

Size 1 fine wire hook

10in(25cm) snood

2oz(60g) lead

Size 1 fine wire hook

The prime bait for dabs is peeler crab, which should be cut into sections to provide neat, small hook baits.

By cracking the shell on the claws and legs, the flesh can be removed to make the bait supply last longer.

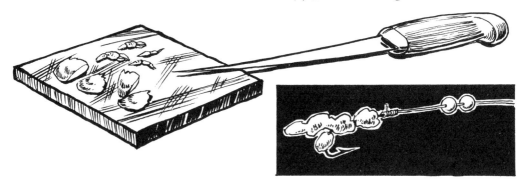

Dabs like a clean, sandy bottom, preferably on the slopes of a sandbank. Neap tides provide the ideal conditions for this sweet-tasting little fish.

Coloured beads set above the hook create an extra attraction.

Sole are also, occasionally, taken with this tackle, especially if the fishing is being carried out after dark.

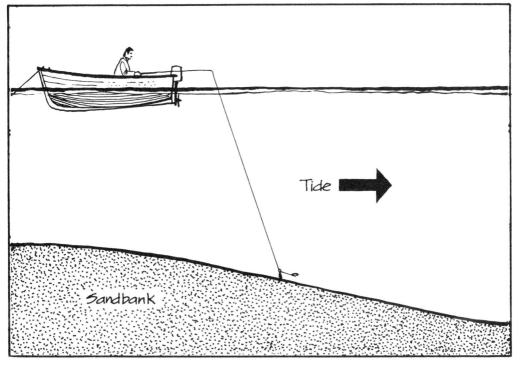

Tide ➡

Sandbank

Fishing for flounders and plaice

Flounders are far more common than plaice but often share the same feeding grounds. Tackle can be identical for both species.

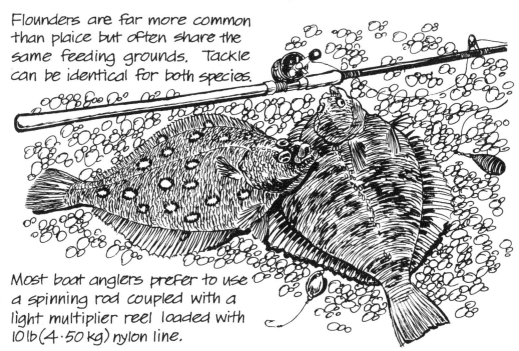

Most boat anglers prefer to use a spinning rod coupled with a light multiplier reel loaded with 10 lb (4.50 kg) nylon line.

Terminal tackle

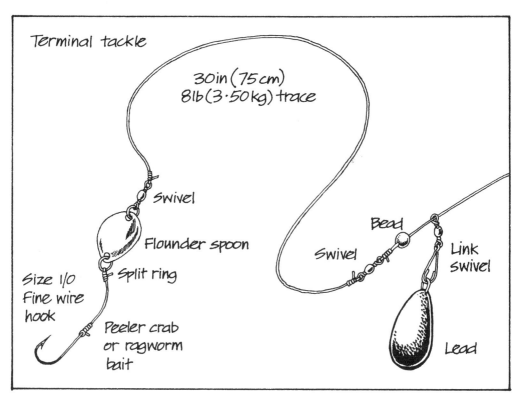

30 in (75 cm)
8 lb (3.50 kg) trace

Swivel

Flounder spoon

Split ring

Size 1/0
Fine wire
hook

Peeler crab
or ragworm
bait

Bead

Swivel

Link swivel

Lead

Three ways of using the rig.

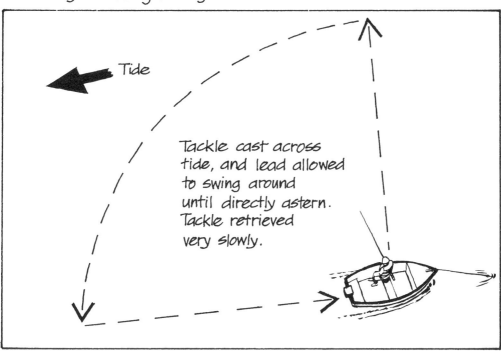

Tide

Tackle cast across
tide, and lead allowed
to swing around
until directly astern.
Tackle retrieved
very slowly.

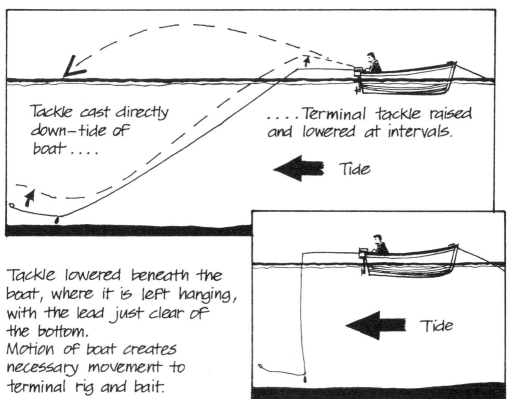

Tackle cast directly
down-tide of
boat . . . .

. . . . Terminal tackle raised
and lowered at intervals.

Tide

Tackle lowered beneath the
boat, where it is left hanging,
with the lead just clear of
the bottom.
Motion of boat creates
necessary movement to
terminal rig and bait.

Tide

Fishing for dogfish

This scavenger hunts in packs, and sport can be fast and furious if a concentration of the species is located. They feed mainly over rough ground, where the angler should present the bait right on the bottom.

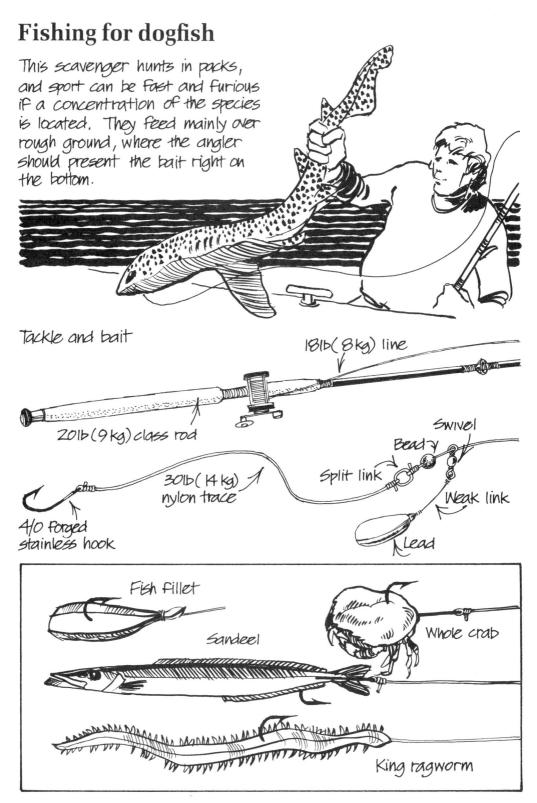

Tackle and bait

18lb (8 kg) line

20lb (9 kg) class rod

Swivel

Bead

Split link

30lb (14 kg) nylon trace

Weak link

4/0 forged stainless hook

Lead

Fish fillet

Sandeel

Whole crab

King ragworm

The best time for 'dogs' is after dark or during poor light.

Remember! The dogfish is related to the shark family and the skin is very rough. Always wear a thick leather glove when handling these fish.

Large dogfish can weigh as much as 15lb (7kg).

Safety in the boat

Even in the comparatively sheltered waters encountered by the inshore boat angler, the sea can often be a very fickle and dangerous place. Every angler should be prepared for any emergency by making sure, before putting to sea, that all the items shown here are on board.

Tool kit and spare spark plug

First aid kit

Flares

C B Radio

Life jacket

Compass

Baler

Spare anchor

When fishing from a small craft it is advisable to 'trip' the anchor, so that in the event of the anchor jamming in rocks it can be pulled free.

Remain seated and pull from the bows.

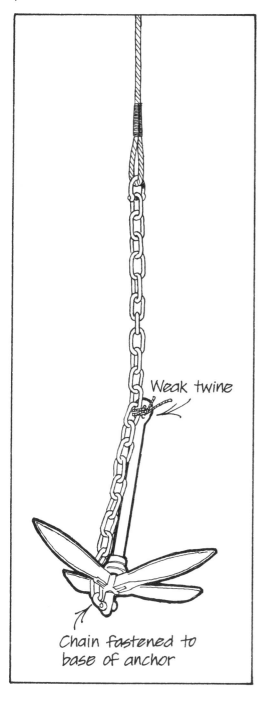

Weak twine

Chain fastened to base of anchor

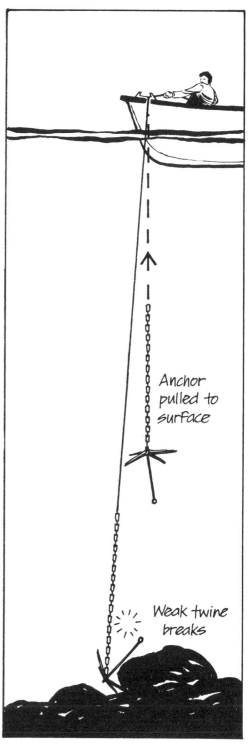

Anchor pulled to surface

Weak twine breaks

Pinpointing a mark

If a good fishing spot has been located in sight of land, the angler will, no doubt, wish to return at some other date, to enjoy further sport. Providing there are recognizable landmarks, this should be an easy matter of taking a couple of bearings.

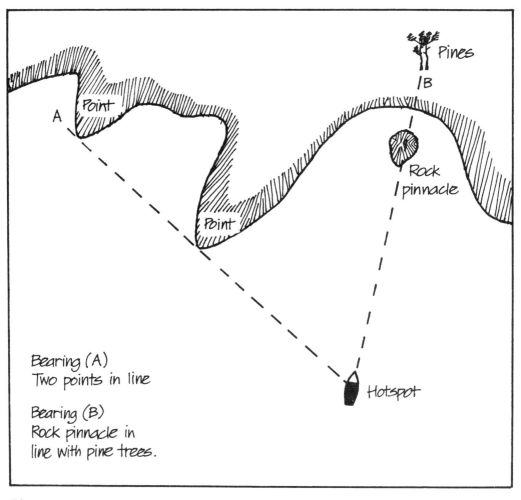

Bearing (A)
Two points in line

Bearing (B)
Rock pinnacle in line with pine trees.

Tackle maintenance

Salt water causes corrosion to metal surfaces. Reels and rod fittings both contain metal, and both items are expensive. After every fishing session, wash rod and reel under cold, fresh water.

Spray reels with water repellant, and oil and grease necessary points.

Every so often, strip reels down completely and clean the internal mechanism, re-grease and re-assemble.

By following this simple procedure your reel will last a lifetime and function efficiently to give you trouble-free fishing.

Hook sizes and anatomy

4

2

1

1/0

2/0

3/0

4/0

5/0

6/0

7/0

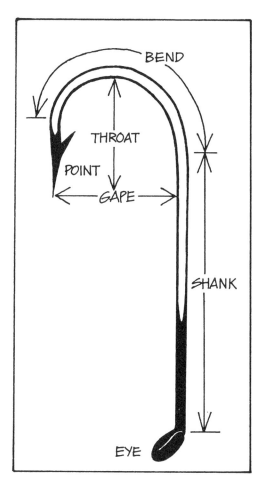

BEND

THROAT

POINT

GAPE

SHANK

EYE

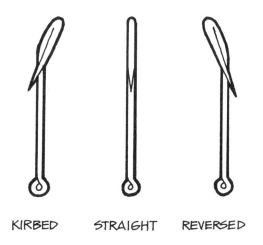

KIRBED   STRAIGHT   REVERSED

Knots

TUCKED FULL BLOOD KNOT
For joining line of widely-differing thickness. The thinner line must be doubled at the tying end, and taken around the thicker line twice as many times as the thicker line is turned around it.

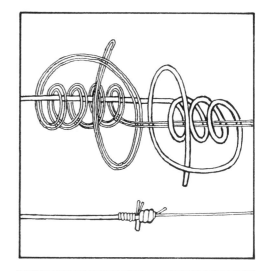

PALOMAR KNOT
A simple, neat and efficient knot for connecting a hook to nylon line.

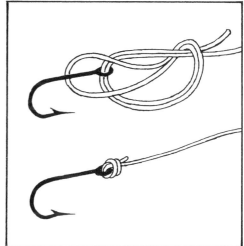

UNI KNOT
One of the strongest knots in use today. This is another good knot for connecting lead to a shock leader. It is also very popular among deep-sea anglers.

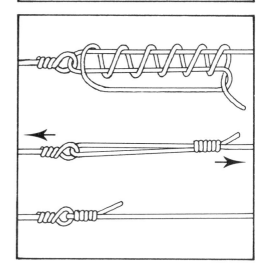

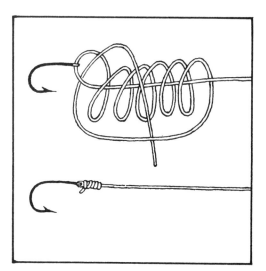

TUCKED HALF-BLOOD KNOT
For joining hooks, swivels and leads to line. Properly tied, this is a safe knot for joining a sinker to the end of a shock leader. Serious injuries have been inflicted by leads flying off during the cast. Frequently check the knot joining lead to leader.

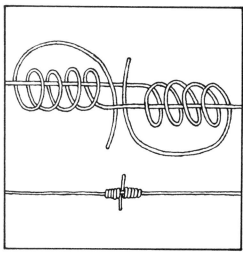

FULL BLOOD KNOT
The best knot for joining two lengths of line of the same, or similar, thickness.

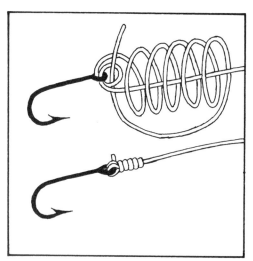

CLINCHED HALF-BLOOD KNOT
A better knot for use on heavier—gauged hooks.

Knots

DROPPER LOOP KNOT
The only knot for creating a connecting point for paternoster snoods.

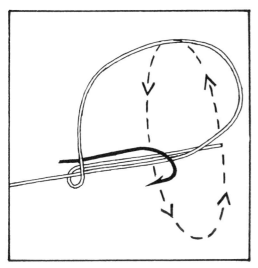

STOP KNOT
A very useful knot when fishing with a sliding float. Leave both tag ends very long for maximum efficiency.

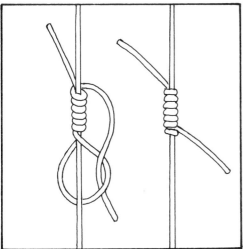

SNELL KNOT
Mainly used for the construction of mackerel feathers.